PIZZA
COOKBOOK

A QUINTET BOOK

ISBN: 0–7858–0507–9

This book was designed and produced by
Quintet Publishing Limited

Art Director: Peter Bridgewater
Editor: Nicholas Law
Photographer: John Heseltine
Jacket Design: Nik Morley

Typeset in Great Britain by
Central Southern Typesetters, Eastbourne

Produced in Australia by Griffin Colour

Published by Chartwell Books
A Division of Book Sales, Inc.
P.O. Box 7100
Edison, New Jersey 08818–7100

PIZZA
COOKBOOK

MYRA STREET

CHARTWELL
BOOKS, INC.

Contents

INTRODUCTION

Wholewheat pepper and caper pizza

The pizza originated in Naples, an invention of Neapolitan bakers for the poverty-stricken inhabitants of the back streets of the city, to make a little food stretch a long way. Because it is still a cheap and cheerful way to eat, the pizza has become even more popular in other countries than it is in Italy and there are pizza restaurants all over the world.

The Neapolitan pizza is made with fresh tomatoes, oregano, anchovy fillets, mozzarella cheese and olive oil. There are now countless toppings for pizzas and making them at home is an excellent way of utilizing fresh vegetables, meats and cheese to add variety to family meals.

Salami, chicken, bacon, smoked hams and spicy sausages can all be used as toppings with different cheeses on a tomato base.

Fish pizzas can be flavoured with anchovies, clams, mussels, prawns, shrimps, and tuna fish on tomatoes and herbs.

Pizzas are also a great boon to vegetarians as a tomato base is ideal with mushrooms, green, red or yellow peppers, aubergines (eggplant), artichoke hearts, sweetcorn (corn), herbs, black or green olives with or without cheese according to preference.

Professional pizza chefs hurl the dough in the air to achieve the correct thickness but at home the dough can be rolled and moulded without this particular technique. The authentic pizza texture imparted by a brick-built pizza oven cannot be recreated exactly at home. Homemade pizzas are therefore bound to be slightly different, but they are still very good and you can be sure of delicious toppings. The deep pan pizza is much easier to copy at home with the aid of a flan ring or sandwich cake tin.

Bake your own pizzas to suit your family's tastes and you will discover, as have the Neapolitan bakers, that a little does indeed go a long way. Small children, teenagers and adults are enthusiastic pizza-eaters and pizzas are therefore always popular. A glass of wine and a pizza are really only the equivalents of a beer and a sandwich, but they always seem more exciting.

Making bread dough for pizzas is straightforward providing the cook who is not familiar with yeast cookery keeps the following notes in mind when using the recipes. Enough time must be allowed for the dough to prove, but during this time it requires no attention and other work may be done.

FLOUR

Strong white flour is best for bread doughs as it has a high gluten content which helps to give the texture and volume associated with bread doughs. As a warm atmosphere suits yeast particularly well, it is a good idea to sieve flour into a slightly warmed bowl.

Many people prefer whole grain flours today and enjoy wholewheat pizzas. It must be noted that a mixture using only wholewheat flour will be fairly solid to eat but this is a matter of for individual taste. A mixture of strong white flour and wholewheat gives a more digestible pizza.

YEAST

is a living organism which is used as a raising agent in bread doughs. Yeast feeds on sugars and multiplies in warm moist conditions releasing carbon dioxide which expands when heated to give dough its characteristic spongy texture. However yeast can also be killed by excessive heat and it is essential that the yeast mixture be the correct temperature around 43°C/110°F. Yeast wakes up gradually — do not be too impatient.

SALT

contributes to the flavour of the dough but it can also kill yeast cells. Only use the recommended amounts and do not allow the salt to come into direct contact with the yeast. The salt should be sieved or mixed with the flour. The proportion is usually 2 tsp to each 4½ cups/450 g/1 lb flour used.

SUGAR

if creamed with yeast can kill it; therefore it is essential not to add more than the amounts given in the recipes. Sugar added to the measured liquid and dissolved will be enough to activate the yeast without overpowering it.

LIQUIDS

used in yeast mixtures are either milk or water or a combination of the two. It is most important for the liquid to be the correct temperature. If it is warmer than 43°C/110°F it will destroy yeast cells. Try putting a finger in the water; if it feels warm, cool it slightly. Most beginners make the liquid too hot.

It is also important to measure liquids and put in less than the recipe states as more liquid can always be added but too much cannot be removed. Add the last of it carefully to obtain a slightly sticky but not wet dough. The mixture will firm to an elastic consistency as it is kneaded. It is this process which develops the gluten in the flour to give the texture.

RISING TIMES

It is very difficult to give the precise time required for activating yeast — it all depends on the ambient temperature. In cold surroundings yeast grows but only slowly.

In a warm place in front of a central heating radiator or warm cupboard it will take about an hour. At room temperature dough can take up to 2 hours to rise. In a cool room it will rise in about 5 hours and in a refrigerator in about 12 hours.

These rising times are useful to remember as the process can be organized around other activities.

MAKING PIZZA DOUGH

ASSEMBLING INGREDIENTS FOR DOUGH

1 Measure all ingredients accurately. Sieve flour.

2 On the right of the board there is fresh yeast which can be bought from some bakers, delicatessens and health food shops.

3 On the left of the board the jug contains dried yeast mixed with liquid being left to ferment for 15 minutes.

ADDING THE YEAST MIXTURE TO THE FLOUR

Make a well in the centre of the flour, add oil and cover with a little flour. Pour in the yeast liquid and the remaining liquid.

MIXING THE DOUGH

Use a palette knife or plastic spatula to mix the dough until all the liquid has been absorbed to make a firm but pliable dough. Add liquid carefully at the end to prevent the dough becoming too sticky. If you add too much liquid, you will have to work in more flour which spoils the dough's consistency.

KNEADING THE DOUGH

When the dough is mixed turn onto a floured board and knead vigorously for 10 minutes. The kneading motion is done by pushing with the heel of the hand and turning the dough over continuously until it is smooth.

PROVING THE DOUGH

Place in a bowl which has been lightly floured or in an oiled plastic bag. If using a bowl, cover with plastic wrap or place inside a plastic bag or cover with a clean tea towel. This careful covering of the dough is to stop cooling air currents from interfering with the rising processs. The dough (right) has risen and the covering just removed. Proving at this stage will take approximately an hour in a warm room, longer if the room is cool.

KNOCKING BACK (PUNCHING DOWN) THE RISEN DOUGH

Turn the risen dough onto a floured board and knead again until the pockets of gas which are now unevenly distributed are knocked out (punched down). The dough is now smooth, firm and elastic.

For speed, many recipes shape the pizzas at this stage but for a really delicious home-made pizza use the Pizza Dough 2 recipe. The second rising develops the real texture and the extra time is worthwhile.

— seems to need more water - try in mixer next time

PIZZA DOUGH 1

Ingredients

1 tbsp/15 g/½ oz fresh or 2 tsp dried yeast
½ cup/115 ml/4 fl oz slightly warmed water
1 tsp sugar
4½ cups/450 g/1 lb strong plain flour
1 tsp salt
1 tbsp oil

To prepare

1 Blend fresh yeast with a little of the measured water which has the sugar dissolved in it. For dried yeast dissolve 1 tsp sugar in one third of the measured water, sprinkle the yeast onto the water and whisk. Leave to stand for 10-15 minutes until frothy.

2 Sieve the flour and salt into a bowl and make a well in the centre, add the oil, sprinkle over with a little flour.

3 Add the yeast liquid and most of the remaining water and mix well until the dough starts to leave the side of the bowl. If it seems too stiff add the remaining liquid slowly.

4 Turn onto a lightly floured board and knead well for about 10 minutes. When the dough is elastic and smooth place in a floured bowl and cover with a tea towel or plastic wrap. Alternatively leave it to rise in an oiled plastic bag until it has doubled in size. This will take approximately an hour in a warm kitchen.

5 The dough can then be knocked back (punched down) and shaped for pizzas.

The dough with two risings in my opinion gives the better home-made pizza.

Makes 2 × 30-cm (12-in) pizzas or 3 × 20-cm (8-in) pizzas

PIZZA DOUGH 2

Ingredients

4½ cups/1.4 kg/3 lb flour
1 tbsp/30 g/1 oz salt
4 tbsp/50 g/2 oz fresh or 2 tbsp/25 g/1 oz dried yeast
2¼ cups/500 ml/18 fl oz water
½ cup/125 ml/4 fl oz milk
2 tbsp oil

To prepare

1 Sieve the flour into a large bowl and make a well in the centre.

2 Add the yeast by crumbling into the centre of the well.

3 Make sure that the water and milk are just body temperature and pour most of the mixture into the well with the yeast.

4 Dissolve the salt in a little of the remaining liquid. Add oil. Pour them into mixture.

5 Knead well for about 10 minutes by hand. Place back in the bowl or in an oiled large plastic bag.

6 Allow to stand in a warm kitchen for about an hour or until the dough has doubled in size.

7 Knock back (punch down) the dough by kneading well with the heel of the hand.

8 Replace the dough in the bowl or bag and allow to rise again for a further hour.

Makes 4 × 30-cm (12-in) oblong or round pizzas

WHOLEWHEAT PIZZA DOUGH

Ingredients

1 tbsp/15 g/½ oz fresh or 3 level tsp dried yeast
⅝ cup/150 ml/¼ pt slightly warmed water
1 tsp sugar
2¼ cups/225 g/8 oz wholewheat flour
2¼ cups/225 g/8 oz plain flour
1 tsp salt
1 tbsp oil

To prepare

1 Cream fresh yeast with 3 tbsp measured liquid in which the sugar has been dissolved. Dried yeast should be mixed with one-third of the measured liquid with sugar dissolved in it, whisked and allowed to stand in a warm room for 10-15 minutes until frothy.

2 Pour the wholewheat flour into a bowl, sieve the white flour and salt on top and mix well.

3 Make a well in the centre of the flour, pour in the oil, and cover with flour. Add the yeast mixture and most of the liquid. Mix well until dough leaves the side of the bowl, adding the remaining liquid if mixture is too dry. You may need a little extra liquid to take up the wholewheat flour but do not add too much.

4 Turn onto a floured board and knead well until a smooth elastic dough is made after about 10 minutes.

5 Put back into the bowl and cover with plastic wrap or place the dough in an oiled plastic bag. Allow to rise in a warm kitchen until doubled in size, this will take 45 minutes to an hour. Knock back (punch down) the dough and shape as required.

Makes 2 × 30-cm (12-in) or 3 × 20-cm (8-in) pizzas

PIZZAS

Deep Dish Mozzarella and Salami Pizza

Deep Dish Ham and Mushroom Pizza

Deep Dish Artichoke Heart and Bacon Pizza

Neopolitan Pizza

Tomato and Green Olive Pizza

Deep Dish Mushroom and Prosciutto Pizza

Four Cheese Pizza

Wholewheat Pepper and Caper Pizza

Pizza Sicilana

Family Pizza

Wholewheat Aubergine (Eggplant) and
Mozzarella Pizza

Individual Blue Cheese Pizza

Potato Pan Pizza

Tuna Scone Pizza

Quick Supper Pizza

Wholewheat Scone Pizza

Deep dish mozzarella and salami pizza

DEEP DISH MOZZARELLA AND SALAMI PIZZA

Ingredients
2¼ cups/225 g/8 oz flour made into pizza dough
Topping
1½ cups/425 g/15 oz canned tomatoes, drained
2 tsp oil
1 tsp origanum
12 slices Italian salami
12 thin slices mozzarella cheese
2 tbsp parmesan cheese
salt and freshly ground pepper
½ cup/50 g/2 oz black olives
Oven temperature 220°C/425°F/Gas 7

To prepare

1 Make the dough and allow to rise. Knock back and shape in 2 × 20-cm (8-in) flan rings (pie plates) placed on a baking sheet or sandwich cake pans.

2 Mash down the tomatoes and add a little of the drained juice.

3 Brush the dough with oil and arrange the tomatoes on the bottom.

4 Roll the salami into rounds. Sprinkle a little parmesan cheese on the tomato and then the origanum. Arrange the salami rolls.

5 Place the slices of mozzarella cheese alternately with salami. Season well.

6 Sprinkle on the remaining Parmesan and decorate the whole with black olives.

7 Brush over with oil and cook in a hot oven for 20 minutes. Reduce the heat to 190°C/375°F/Gas 5 for a further 5-10 minutes.

Makes 2 × 20-cm (8-in) pizzas

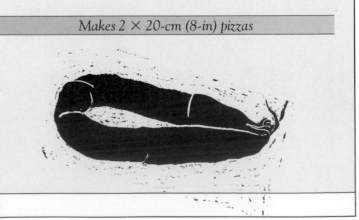

DEEP DISH HAM AND MUSHROOM PIZZA

Ingredients
2¼ cups/225 g/8 oz flour made into pizza dough
1 tbsp oil
1¼ cups/300 ml/½ pt well flavoured bechamel sauce
salt and freshly ground pepper
1½ cups/425 g/15 oz canned tomatoes, drained
½ tsp origanum
6 slices of cooked ham
2 cups/100 g/4 oz mushrooms, washed and sliced
1 cup/100 g/4 oz mozzarella cheese, thinly sliced
Oven temperature 210°C/425°F/Gas 7

To prepare

1 Shape the risen dough.

2 Brush over the dough with oil and divide the bechamel sauce between the two bases.

3 Arrange half the sliced mushrooms on the bechamel sauce.

4 Chop the canned tomatoes and divide between the two bases. Season well and sprinkle with origanum.

5 Cut the slices of ham in two and roll them up, placing 6 rolls on each pizza alternating with thin slices of mozzarella cheese. Garnish with sliced mushrooms.

6 Bake in a hot oven for 15 minutes and then reduce the heat to 190°C/375°F/Gas 5 for a further 10 minutes.

These pizzas make a very substantial meal; two of them should serve four average appetites.

Makes 2 × 20-cm (8-in) pizzas

DEEP DISH ARTICHOKE HEART AND BACON PIZZA

Ingredients
2¼ cups/225 g/8 oz flour made into pizza dough
1 tbsp olive oil
1¼ cups/300 ml/½ pt pomodoro sauce
1 can artichoke hearts
12 slices bacon
1 tbsp parmesan cheese
1 tbsp freshly chopped basil or parsley leaves
Oven temperature 210°C/425°F/Gas 7

To prepare

1 Shape the risen dough into flan rings (pie plates) or sandwich cake pans (tins).

2 Brush over the dough with the oil and divide the pomodoro sauce between the two bases.

3 Drain the artichoke hearts.

4 Roll up the slices of bacon and cook under the grill (broiler) or in the oven for a few minutes.

5 Sprinkle the pizzas with parmesan cheese and herbs.

6 Arrange the artichoke hearts alternately with the bacon rolls. Brush over with the remaining oil.

7 Cook in a hot oven for 15-20 before reducing the heat to medium (190°C/375°F/Gas 5) for a further 5 minutes.

Makes 2 × 20-cm (8-in) pizzas

NEAPOLITAN PIZZA

Ingredients
2¼ cups/225 g/8 oz flour made into pizza dough
1 tbsp olive oil
1 clove garlic, crushed
6 tomatoes, skinned and sliced
½ tsp origanum
4 chopped basil leaves
Oven temperature 220°C/450°F/Gas 7-8

To prepare

1 Take the 2¼ cups/225 g/8 oz portion of dough and roll into a round shape, kneading the round out to the large 30-cm (12-in) size with floured knuckles. Make sure that it is not too thick. Any left-over dough can be allowed to rise and cooked as a bread roll.

A large flan tin (pie plate) is ideal for this type of pizza but it shapes well on a greased baking tray.

2 Brush over the dough with the olive oil and rub over the whole surface with the well crushed clove of garlic.

3 Arrange the tomatoes over the surface and sprinkle with herbs. Fresh parsley may be used if basil is unobtainable. Season well.

4 Place in a hot oven for 20-25 minutes.

This is the basic tomato pizza but most people prefer to add extra ingredients.

Makes 1 × 30-cm (12-in) pizza

TOMATO AND GREEN OLIVE PIZZA

Make as above but add ⅓ cup/50 g/2 oz grated parmesan cheese and ¼ cup/25 g/1 oz stoned green olives.

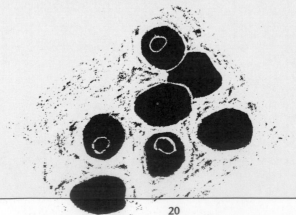

PIZZAS

DEEP DISH MUSHROOM AND PROSCIUTTO PIZZA

Ingredients
2¹/4 cups/225 g/8 oz wholewheat flour made into dough
Topping
1 tbsp oil
1¹/2 cups/425 g/15 oz canned tomatoes, drained
4 tomatoes, skinned and peeled
1 tsp origanum
2 tbsp parmesan cheese
6 cups/350 g/12 oz mushrooms, washed and sliced
8 slices thin smoked ham (prosciutto)
salt and freshly ground pepper
Oven temperature 220°C/425°F/Gas 7

To prepare

1 Shape the dough as for deep dish pizza.

2 Paint the shaped dough with a pastry brush dipped in oil.

3 Arrange the tomatoes on the bases of the pizza dough. Sprinkle with origanum and salt and pepper.

4 Sprinkle half the cheese over the tomato mixture.

5 Melt the butter and the remaining oil in a frying pan and allow the mushrooms to cook over a low heat for about 4 minutes.

6 Spread the mushrooms on top of the pizzas and arrange the ham on top. Sprinkle with the remaining cheese.

7 Cook in a hot oven for 15 minutes, before turning the oven down to 190°C/375°F/Gas 5 for the last 10 minutes.

Makes 2 × 20-cm (8-in) pizzas

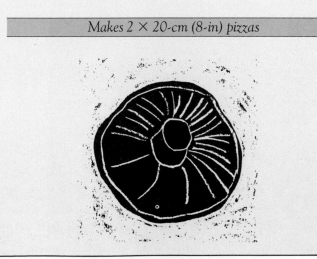

FOUR CHEESE PIZZA

Make the Neapolitan pizza but substitute 4 different cheeses for parmesan. This pizza has ¼ cup/25 g/1 oz each of mozzarella cheese, gruyere cheese, blue cheese and grated cheddar. It is an excellent way to use up small pieces of cheese.

Four cheese pizza

WHOLEWHEAT PEPPER AND CAPER PIZZA

Ingredients

2¼ cups/225 g/8 oz wholewheat flour made into pizza

1 tbsp oil

1½ cups/425 g/15 oz canned tomatoes

½ tsp fresh or ¼ tsp dried thyme

3 cups/175 g/6 oz mushrooms, washed and sliced

1 red pepper, seeded

1 tbsp capers, chopped

salt and freshly ground pepper

2 tbsp parmesan cheese

Oven temperatures 220°C/425°F/Gas 7

To prepare

1 Shape the dough into 2 × 20-cm (8-in) pizzas and brush with oil.

2 Drain and chop the tomatoes, mix with the thyme and spread on the pizza bases. Arrange the mushrooms on the two bases and sprinkle with chopped capers. Season well.

3 Sprinkle with grated cheese and arrange strips of red pepper on top. Bake for 15 minutes in a hot oven and then reduce the temperature to 190°C/375°F/Gas 5 for another 10 minutes.

Makes 2 × 20-cm (8-in) pizzas

PIZZA SICILIANA

Ingredients

2¼ cups/225 g/8 oz flour made into risen pizza dough

⅝ cup/150 ml/¼ pt tomato sauce

4 tomatoes, skinned and sliced

½ tsp oregano

salt and freshly ground pepper

⅓ cup/50 g/2 oz parmesan cheese

1 can anchovies

good ½ cup/75 g/3 oz black olives

Oven temperature 220°C/425°F/Gas 7

To prepare

1 Shape the dough into a rectangular shape 30 cm (12 in) × 20 cms (8 in) or use a flan tin (pie plate) or large swiss roll (jelly roll) pan.

2 Paint the dough with a pastry brush dipped in oil and then cover the surface with the tomato sauce.

3 Place the sliced tomatoes on top and sprinkle with oregano and seasoning.

4 Sprinkle with parmesan cheese.

5 Drain the can of anchovies and arrange the halved fillets in a lattice design. Place an olive in the centre of each lattice.

6 Paint over with the remaining oil and bake in a hot oven for 15 minutes. Then turn the heat down to 190°C/375°F/Gas 5 for a further 10 minutes.

Serves 2-4

Make the pizza up as for Siciliana as far as painting the dough with oil and arranging the sauce on top. Add 1 can chopped tomatoes. Dice a green pepper into small pieces, blanch it for 2 minutes and drain it. Scatter the oregano and pepper on the tomato mixture, followed by ¾ cup/75 g/3 oz grated cheddar. Cut 3 pork sausages in pieces diagonally and arrange on the top of the pizza. Cook as described opposite.

WHOLEWHEAT AUBERGINE (EGGPLANT) & MOZZARELLA PIZZA

Ingredients

1 cup/100 g/4 oz flour made into wholewheat pizza dough
2 tbsp oil
1 small aubergine (eggplant), sliced
salt and freshly ground pepper
$5/8$ cup/150 ml/$1/4$ pt tomato sauce
1 small red pepper, seeded
3 stuffed olives, halved
$1/2$ cup/50 g/2 oz mozzarella cheese
Oven temperature 220°C/425°F/Gas 7

To prepare

1 Shape the pizza into a 20-cm (8-in) round and rub a little oil over the dough.

2 Sprinkle the sliced aubergine with salt and allow it to stand for a few minutes.

3 Spread the tomato sauce over the dough.

4 Cut 6 rings of red pepper.

5 Heat the remaining oil in the frying pan. Drain the aubergine slices of juice on kitchen paper and fry for about 30 seconds on each side.

6 Arrange them on the pizza with a ring of red pepper on top and half an olive in the centre. Place the slices of mozzarella between the aubergine slices and cook in a hot oven for 15 minutes. Turn the heat down 190°C/375°F/Gas 5 for the final 10 minutes.

Makes 1 × 20-cm (8-in) pizza

INDIVIDUAL BLUE CHEESE PIZZA

Use 2¼ cups/225 g/8 oz wholewheat flour made into dough shaped into 4 × 10-cm (4-in) flan tins (pie plates)

Rub with oil and spread ⅝ cup/150 ml/¼ pt tomato sauce on the bottom of each. Arrange small pieces of blue cheese in a circle round the outside — the pizzas will take about 1 cup/100 g/4 oz cheese. Garnish with strips of pepper and olives. Cook for 20 minutes in a hot oven.

Individual blue cheese pizza

POTATO PAN PIZZA

Ingredients
Potato Base
2¼ cups/225 g/8 oz cooked, sieved potatoes
2¼ cups/225 g/8 oz plain flour
1 tsp salt
½ level tsp dried mustard
1 tsp mixed herbs
6 tbsp/75 g/3 oz butter
1 egg, beaten
½ cup/50 g/2 oz grated cheese
⅝ cup/150 ml/¼ pt milk
⅝ cup/150 ml/¼ pt oil for frying
Topping
1 onion, peeled and chopped
1½ cups/425 g/15 oz canned tomatoes, drained
1 tsp dried basil
salt and pepper
1½ cups/175 g/6 oz grated cheese
Optional garnish
anchovies, black olives or slices of cooked ham
Oven temperature 190°C/375°F/Gas 5

To prepare

1 Mix the butter with the warm sieved potatoes in a bowl. Weigh the potato after cooking to make sure proportions are correct.

2 Sieve in the flour, salt, dried mustard and herbs. Mix with the egg, add the cheese and make a stiff dough with milk.

3 Turn onto a floured board and divide the mixture into 6. Roll into rounds approximately 12 cm (5 in) in diameter.

4 Heat the oil in a deep frying pan and fry the potato bases until golden brown each side.

5 Arrange on a baking sheet and prepare the filling.

6 Drain the frying pan and clean out with some kitchen paper. Pour back a little of the strained oil and cook the finely chopped onion for 4 minutes over a low heat, add the canned tomatoes and break up in the pan. Season well and mix in the basil.

7 Divide the tomato filling between the potato bases and cover them with cheese. Any other topping can be added at this stage.

8 Cook for 10 minutes or until golden brown in the preheated oven.

Serves 6

TUNA SCONE PIZZA

Ingredients
2¼ cups/225 g/8 oz flour made into scone dough

Topping
1 tsp oil
1½ cups/450 g/1 lb tomatoes, skinned and sliced
1 cup/100 g/4 oz cheddar cheese
scant 1 cup/200 g/7 oz canned tuna fish
½ tsp mixed herbs
salt and pepper
7 black olives
Oven temperature 210°C/425°F/Gas 7

To prepare

1 Make the scone mixture and roll out to a 25-cm (10-in) round.

2 Paint over with oil and arrange the sliced tomatoes. Sprinkle with half the cheese.

3 Arrange the tuna fish evenly around the outside of the pizza and sprinkle all over with mixed herbs. Season well.

4 Finish with a layer of cheese. Arrange the olives in a ring near the centre of the circle.

5 Paint over with oil and cook in a preheated hot oven. Turn the oven down after 10 minutes to 190°C/375°F/Gas 5 for the remaining 15-20 minutes cooking time.

6 Serve immediately.

Serves 2-4

QUICK SUPPER PIZZA

Ingredients
2¼ cups/225 g/8 oz self-raising flour
½ level tsp salt
1 level tsp baking powder
½ level tsp dried mustard
4 tbsp/50 g/2 oz butter
⅝ cup/150 ml/¼ pt milk
Topping
1½ cups/450 g/1 lb tomatoes, peeled and sliced
½ tsp origanum or basil
2 cups/225 g/8 oz cheddar cheese
salt and pepper
8 anchovy fillets
12 black olives
1 tsp oil
Oven temperature 220°C/450°F/Gas 7

To prepare

1 Sieve the flour and salt into a mixing bowl.

2 Cut the butter into small pieces and rub into the flour with the tips of the fingers until the mixture resembles fine breadcrumbs.

3 Add most of the milk and mix to a soft dough. Add the remaining milk unless it will make the dough too sticky.

4 Roll out the dough into a 25-cm (10-in) circle, keeping the shape as round as possible. The bottom of a cake pan can be used as a guide.

5 Sprinkle a little cheese on the scone round, then some slices of tomato with a sprinkling of origanum or basil and a shake of salt and pepper. Sprinkle more cheese on the round, then add the remaining tomatoes, herbs and seasoning. Finish with a layer of grated cheese.

6 Decorate with strips of anchovy and black olives. Paint over with oil.

7 Place in a preheated oven for 8 minutes then turn the heat down to 200°C/400°F/Gas 6 for about 15 minutes until pizza is golden and cooked.
  Serve immediately.

Serves 2-4

WHOLEWHEAT SCONE PIZZA

Ingredients
1¼ cups/125 g/5 oz wholewheat flour
¾ cup/75 g/3 oz plain flour
4 level tsp baking powder
½ tsp salt
3 tbsp/40 g/1½ oz butter
⅝ cup/150 ml/¼ pt milk
Topping
2 tbsp oil
1 onion, peeled and diced
1 pepper, seeded
2 cups/100 g/4 oz mushrooms, washed and sliced
½ cup/50 g/2 oz grated cheese
4 tomatoes, peeled and sliced
1 tsp fresh mixed herbs
Oven temperature 220°C/425°F/Gas 7

To prepare

1 Pour the wholewheat flour into a mixing bowl, sieve the white flour, baking powder and salt into the bowl and mix well.

2 Rub in the butter with the tips of the fingers until the mixture resembles fine breadcrumbs.

3 Add the milk and mix to a soft dough, a further small quantity of milk may be needed to mix the dough to the correct consistency. Turn on to a lightly floured board and knead lightly into a round shape.

4 Roll out into a 25-cm (10-in) round and place on a baking sheet.

5 To start the filling, heat the oil in a frying pan and cook the onions over a low heat for 4 minutes.

6 Cut the pepper into thin rings and blanch in boiling water for 2 minutes. Drain.

7 Add the washed, sliced mushrooms to the onion and allow to cook for a further 2 minutes.

8 Arrange the tomatoes on the scone base and sprinkle with mixed herbs and seasoning.

9 Arrange mushrooms and onions on top of the tomatoes, and sprinkle with cheese. Put the rings of peppers on last.

10 Cook in a preheated oven for 10 minutes reducing the heat to 190°C/375°F/Gas 5 for a further 10 minutes.

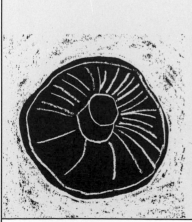

Ingredients

2¼ cups/225 g/8 oz flour made into pizza dough

1 tbsp olive oil

1½ cups/425 g/15 oz canned tomatoes

½ tbsp fresh or ¼ tbsp dried thyme

1½ cups/425g/15 oz fresh mozzarella cheese

1 tbsp fresh or ½ tbsp dried oregano

Oven tempretures 220°C/425°F/Gas 7

To prepare

1 Shape the dough into 2 x 20-cm (8-in) pizzas and brush with the oil.

2 Drain and finely chop the tomatoes, mix with the thyme and spread on the pizza bases.

3 Grate the mozzarella cheese and spread it generously over the top of the tomatoes. Season with the oregano and bake for 15-20 minutes in a hot oven until golden brown.

Makes 2 x 20-cm (8-in) pizzas

Ingredients

2¼ cups/225 g/8 oz flour made into pizza dough

1 tbsp olive oil

1½ cups/425 g/15 oz canned tomatoes

½ tbsp fresh or ¼ tbsp dried oregano

1½ cups/425 g/15 oz fresh mozzarella cheese

6 anchovy fillets

1 tbsp capers, chopped

12 slices of Italian salami

2 cups/100 g/4 oz mushrooms, washed and sliced

12 artichoke hearts

salt and freshly ground pepper

Oven tempretures 220˚C/425˚F/Gas 7

To prepare

1 Preheat the oven. Proceed as though making Pizza Marguerita up to – but not including – the oregano-sprinkling stage.

2 Arrange even quantities of the anchovies, capers, salami, mushrooms and artichoke hearts on top of each pizza.

3 Now season with the oregano and bake for 15-20 minutes in a hot oven until golden brown.

Makes 2 x 20-cm (8-in) pizzas

Ingredients

3½ cups/350 g/12 oz strong white flour
1 cup/100 g/4 oz very fine semolina flour
5 tbsp fresh yeast
⅔ cup/¼ pt olive oil
salt to taste
⅔ cup/¼ pt milk
½ cup/50 g/2 oz green olives
Oven tempretures 200˚C/400˚F/Gas 6

To prepare

1 Sift the two flours together. Mix the yeast with a very little warm water. When it begins to foam, work it into the flours with a quarter of the olive oil and the salt. Blend all the ingredients very thoroughly.

2 Heat the milk. It is hot enough when bubbles begin to show around the edges of the pan.

3 Combine the milk and the flour and yeast mixture – if you have a mixer with a dough hook, so much the better. Fold in the olives.

4 Cover the dough and let it stand in a warm place for about 30 minutes. Then remove and shape into a flat round loaf.

5 Lightly oil a baking sheet with the remaining olive oil and place the loaf on it. Brush the rest generously over the dough.

6 Bake in a preheated oven for 25 minutes until the top is golden brown.

Serves approx. 6

Ingredients
2¼ cups/225 g/8 oz flour made into pizza dough
1 tbsp olive oil
1½ cups/425 g/15 oz canned tomatoes
½ tbsp fresh or ¼ tbsp dried oregano
1½ cups/425 g/15 oz fresh mozzarella cheese
12 anchovy fillets
2 tsp finely chopped basil
2-3 cloves of garlic, finely chopped
salt and freshly ground pepper
Oven tempretures 220°C/425°F/Gas 7

To prepare

1 Preheat the oven. Shape the dough into 2 x 20-cm pizzas and brush with oil.

2 Top with the tomatoes, plenty of pepper, garlic and basil followed by the anchovies and sliced mozzarella cheese. Finally sprinkle olive oil over the top of each pizza.

3 Now season with the oregano and bake for 20-30 minutes in a hot oven until golden brown.

Makes 2 x 20-cm (8-in) pizzas

Ingredients
2¼ cups/225 g/8 oz flour made into pizza dough
1 tbsp olive oil
1 cup/100 g/4 oz concentrated tomato sauce
½ tbsp fresh or ¼ tbsp dried oregano
½ cup/50 g/2 oz black olives
1½ cups/175 g/6 oz cheddar cheese, thinly sliced
1 clove of garlic, finely chopped
Oven tempretures 220°C/425°F/Gas 7

To prepare
1 Preheat the oven. Shape the dough into 4 x 12-cm pizzas and brush with oil.
2. Top with the tomato sauce, oregano, olives and cheese, and sprinkle with the garlic.
3 Bake for 15-20 minutes in a hot oven until the cheese is golden brown and bubbling.

Serves 4

Ingredients

½ cup/100g/4 oz butter, softened

3–6 cloves of garlic, unpeeled

salt and pepper

To prepare

1 Cream the butter until light and fluffy.

2 Blanch the garlic in boiling water for 1 minute, drain and peel.

3 Crush the garlic to a fine paste with a pinch of salt and gradually mix in the softened butter.

4 Season with salt and pepper to taste, wrap in foil and chill until needed.

Ingredients
1 French loaf
Garlic Butter (previous page), softened
5 g/1 tsp mixed fresh herbs, chopped
Oven tempretures 180°C/350°F/Gas 4

To prepare

1 Slice the bread, but not right through the bottom of the loaf.

2 Spread both sides of each slice with the softened Garlic Butter and sprinkle with herbs.

3 Wrap the loaf in foil and heat through in the oven for approximately 20 minutes.

WALDORF SALADS

Ingredients

8 stalks crisp celery

2 rozy-skinned dessert apples

lemon juice

½ cup/50 g/2 oz walnuts

6 tbsp mayonaise

salt and freshly ground black pepper

To prepare

1 Immerse the celery in ice-cold water to freshen it up. Pat dry and slice.

2 Core the apples but do not peel as the color will add contrast to the salad.

3 Slice the apples and sprinkle with lemon juice to prevent discoloring. Toss all the ingredients in the mayonaise and season well.

Serves 2–4

CHICORY AND ALFALFA SALAD

Ingredients

½ small chicory, torn into pieces

1 cup/100 g/4 oz alfalfa sprouts

½ cup/50 g/2 oz small button mushrooms, thinly sliced

½ red bell pepper, sliced

To prepare

1 Arrange the chicory on a large serving plate or 4 individual plates.

2 Mix the alfalfa sprouts, mushrooms and pepper in a bowl.

3 Toss with a salad dressing in the bowl and turn contents out onto the bed of chicory leaves.

Serves 4–6